P9-DED-984

A Rhinoceros Grows Up

by Anastasia Suen ~ illustrated by Michael L. Denman and William J. Huiett

Thanks to our advisers for their expertise, research, and advice:

Randy Rieches, Curator
Zoological Society of San Diego
San Diego Zoo
San Diego, California

Susan Kesselring, M.A., Literacy Educator
Rosemount–Apple Valley–Eagan (Minnesota) School District

Editorial Director: Carol Jones
Managing Editor: Catherine Neitge
Creative Director: Keith Griffin
Editor: Christianne Jones
Story Consultant: Terry Flaherty
Designer: Nathan Gassman
Production Artist: Angela Kilmer
Page Production: Picture Window Books
The illustrations in this book were created with acrylics

Picture Window Books
5115 Excelsior Boulevard, Suite 232
Minneapolis, MN 55416
877-845-8392
www.picturewindowbooks.com

Printed in the United States of America.

Library of Congress Cataloging-in-Publication Data
Suen, Anastasia.
A rhinoceros grows up / by Anastasia Suen ; illustrated by Michael Denman
and William J. Huiett.
p. cm. — (Wild animals)
Includes bibliographical references and index.
ISBN 1-4048-0986-4 (hardcover)
1. Rhinoceroses—Infancy—Juvenile literature. 2. Rhinoceroses—Development—Juvenile
literature. I. Denman, Michael L., ill. II. Huiett, William J., 1943- ill. III. Title.
QL737.U63S84 2006
599.66'8139—dc22
2005004281

Welcome to the world of wild animals! Follow a white rhino as she grows up in Africa. Observe her as she eats, naps, cools off in the mud, and starts a family of her own.

In the tall African grass, a baby rhino is born. The calf snuggles up to her mother. She has two small bumps for horns. As she grows older, her horns will grow.

A female rhino is called a cow.
A male rhino is called a bull.
A baby rhino is called a calf.

Up she goes! The calf stands up shortly after birth. In a few hours, she can walk by herself.

A white rhino calf is almost 2 feet (60 centimeters) tall at birth and weighs about 150 pounds (67.5 kilograms).

The calf stays close to her mother.
She is not strong enough to walk very far.

Munch, munch, munch.
The calf begins to eat grass when
she is a few weeks old.

The calf drinks milk from her mother
for about one to two years.

The word rhinoceros means
nose horn in Greek.

After several weeks, the cow
brings her new calf back to
the herd, or crash.

Two other cows and their calves come out to greet them. The calf does not meet her father. Male rhinos live alone.

Bulls have a large territory with several cows living in it. They do not belong to a herd.

Up and down and side-to-side.
The calf scratches the bugs off her
back by rubbing a tree stump.

A tick bird flies down and lands on the calf's back. The tick bird eats the ticks and other bugs that land on her.

Tick bird is another name for the oxpecker bird. The oxpecker eats the bugs that the rhino cannot reach.

Nap time! It's too hot to eat at noon, so the young rhino naps in the shade. Her mother looks like she is awake, but she naps while standing up.

In the late afternoon, the calf will wake up and start eating again. Then she will go to the water hole for a drink.

Rhinos eat during the cooler parts of the day—evening, night, and early morning.

15

After the calf drinks at the water hole, she follows her mother to the mud wallows. The cow rolls in the wallow at the edge of the water hole and covers herself with mud.

When her mother finishes, the calf rolls in the mud, too. The calf rolls and rolls until she is covered with mud from head to toe.

The mud in the wallows cools down the rhinos and prevents sunburn. It also keep the bugs from biting.

The young calf is now three years old and all grown up. She is ready to leave her mother. She is also ready to mate and have babies of her own.

The young cow forms a herd with several other young cows. They eat and go to the water hole together every day.

Young bulls also form a herd when they are three years old. They will establish their own territories when they are older.

19

The young cow mates with a bull. About 17 months later, her baby is born. When her calf is strong enough, the young cow will take him back to the crash.

When the new calf grows up, he will be one of the largest animals in the world. He will mate, and a new calf will be born in the African grass.

Adult white rhino bulls are 6 feet (180 centimeters) tall and can weigh as much as 4,500 pounds (2,025 kilograms).

Rhinoceros Diagram

① **FEET** Rhinos have three toes on their hooved feet. They walk on the middle toe.

② **NOSE** Adult rhinos rely on their sense of smell to tell them where they are going.

③ **HORNS** A rhino's horn is made of keratin, just like your fingernails.

④ **SKIN** The skin of a rhinoceros is about .5 to .75 inches (1.27 to 1.9 centimeters) thick.

Map

There are five types of rhinos. They live in Africa and Asia.
The rhinos in this book are white rhinos. They live in Africa.

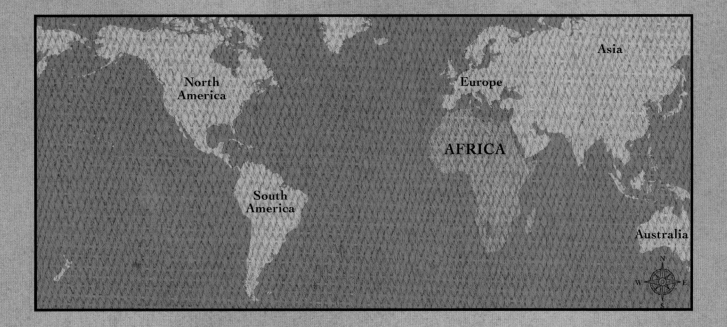

Glossary

bull—an adult male rhino
calf—a young rhino
cow—an adult female rhino
crash—a group, or herd, of rhinos that live together
territory—the place an animal claims as its own
wallows—the mud at the edge of the water hole

To Learn More

At the Library

Cole, Melissa S. *Rhinos*. San Diego: Blackbirch Press, 2002.
Kendell, Patricia. *Rhinos*. Chicago: Raintree, 2004.
Schaefer, Lola M. *Rhinos: Horn-Faced Chargers*. Mankato, Minn.:
Bridgestone Books, 2002.

On the Web

FactHound offers a safe, fun way to find Web sites related to this book. All of the sites on FactHound have been researched by our staff. *www.facthound.com*

1. Visit the FactHound home page.

2. Enter a search word related to this book, or type in this special code: 1404809864

3. Click on the FETCH IT button.

Your trusty FactHound will fetch the best sites for you!

Index

Look for all of the books in the Wild Animals series:

A Baboon Grows Up   A Rhinoceros Grows Up
A Hippopotamus Grows Up   A Tiger Grows Up
A Lion Grows Up   An Elephant Grows Up